TREASURE OF THE Heart

The Ultimate Drive to Living the Faith

TREASURE OF THE Heart
The Ultimate Drive to Living the Faith

Fr. Chinedu Enuh

TREASURE OF THE HEART
The Ultimate Drive to Living the Faith

Copyright © 2024 by Chinedu Enuh

ISBN: 9798332935541

All Rights Reserved.

No part of this publication may be reproduced, distributed, or transmitted in any form or by any means, including photocopying, recording, or any other electronic or mechanical methods, without the prior written permission of the publisher, except in the case of brief quotations embodied in critical reviews and certain other noncommercial uses permitted by copyright law.

Published by:
Gamechangers Media
Tel: +447771021026
Email: gamechangersmedialtd@gmail.com

To all those suffering, persecuted, hated, and yet are faithfully striving to be true to their faith, deep convictions, and to themselves.

ACKNOWLEDGMENTS

"Blessed be the God and Father of our Lord Jesus Christ, who has blessed us in Christ with every spiritual blessing in the heavenly places" (Ephesians 1:3). It is indeed a testament to God's faithfulness and grace that this work has come to fruition. I am reminded that "every good and perfect gift comes from above, coming down from the Father of lights" (James 1:17). To God be the glory!

I extend my heartfelt gratitude to the individuals who shared with me their inspiring stories of faith and perseverance in the face of adversity. Your courage and trust (in sharing your experiences with me) have been a privilege and a blessing. May your testimonies continue to inspire and encourage many.

I also express my sincere thanks to those who helped with the initial and final editorial work. Your expertise, attention to detail, and sacrifice have been invaluable. May God reward your efforts and bless you richly.

Overall, may this book be a testament to the power and grace of God, and may it bring glory to Him alone.

CONTENTS

Dedication	v
Acknowledgments	vi
Foreword	ix
Chapter 1: Treasure of the Heart	1
Chapter 2: Love in Our Hearts as a Drive for Holiness	15
Chapter 3: Implications of the Imitation of Christ	29
Chapter 4: The Christian Faith as a Scandal of Perfect Love	39
Chapter 5: The Scandal of Perfect Love	66
Chapter 6: The Christian Waiting	90
Conclusion	101
References	105

FOREWORD

As I read *Treasure of the Heart,* the thought occurred to me that it was the kind of book you could encourage a retreatant or person who was about to spend time in prayer to read in the expectation that it would lead him or her to a spiritual and enlightening response. I think I know why this may be so. Speaking to Daughters of Charity about two kinds of knowing, St Vincent de Paul said, "A theologian who has only his own special theological knowledge speaks of God in the way his subject has taught him; but a person of prayer speaks of him in quite a different way. And the difference between the two, arises from this, that the one speaks of him through acquired knowledge, and the other through infused knowledge, full of love, so that the theologian in this respect, is not the most learned, and he or she should be silent when a person of prayer is present." It is clear from reading Fr Chinedu's excellent book that instead of writing as a result of acquired knowledge of an academic kind, he writes as a result of infused knowledge of the contemplative nature. While reading this well written book, a number of points stood out for me.

Firstly, St Paul stated in Eph 4:15 that we should "speak the truth in love." The truth without love is harsh and even cruel, while love without truth is sentimentality. Speaking about his ideal, Fr Chinedu says, "The Holy Spirit is gentleness but also the Spirit of truth. This means that the truth is communicated in gentleness. Yet it does not mean that some truths of the Christian faith will not be offensive, at least at the initial stage of conveying them." Over and over again, he quotes relevant scripture texts to ground the points he wants to make. Having explained their meaning, he demonstrates their relevance by relating them to modern life. In the course of doing so, Fr Chinedu shows how a good deal of current thinking and practice fails to measure up to the word and will of God. While he points out these anomalies in a perceptive and challenging manner, he does so in a non-judgemental, non-condemnatory way.

Secondly, the book's central theme is focused on the importance of aspirations, and transcendental desires as the energising factor in the Christian thirst for holiness. They in a sense are the treasure of the heart in so far as they impel a person toward the person and love of God. In asserting this, Fr Chinedu is echoing a statement of St Augustine, "The entire life of a good Christian is in fact an exercise of holy desire. You do not yet see what you long for, but the very act of desiring prepares you, so that when he comes you may see and be utterly satisfied." Ultimately, we seek to encounter and know the God of love and the love of God.

Thirdly, rather than avoiding the problematic topic of suffering in the Christian life, *Treasure of the Heart* shows in an illuminating way, especially in chapter four, how Jesus has shown us that in our sinful world, love and sacrificial suffering are inextricably linked. While reading Fr Chinedu's examination of the scandal of the cross and the role of suffering in the lives of those who love God, I was reminded of something that psychiatrist Viktor Frankl wrote, "In some ways suffering ceases to be suffering at the moment it finds a meaning, such as the meaning of a sacrifice." If sacrificial suffering is an expression of love it ceases to be mind numbingly absurd and becomes suffused with a sense of meaning and purpose. As St Paul stated in 2 Cor 1:4, "God comforts us in all our suffering, so that we may be able to comfort others in all their suffering, as we ourselves are being comforted by God." As Fr Chinedu says, we are wounded healers, in whose lives God's power is perfected in and through our weakness (cf. 2 Cor 12:9).

Fourthly, *Treasure of the Heart* concludes with the tension between the is and the not yet nature of the Christian life. In a way it is about the fact that no matter how much we receive from the Lord, there is always so much more to desire. As St Catherine of Sienna prayed, "You are a mystery as deep as the sea; the more I search, the more I find, and the more I find the more I search for You. But I can never be satisfied; what I receive will ever leave me **desiring** more. When You fill my soul, I have an ever-greater hunger, and I grow more famished for Your light." Talking about discerning true from false desires, Pope St Gregory the Great wrote, "Holy desires grow with delay: if they fade through delay, they are no desires at all." One could say that there is no growth or blessing in the

Christian life without an authentic preceding desire. The deeper and stronger the desire the greater the openness to future growth and blessing.

I really enjoyed reading this book. It is a credit to the author who grew up in Nigeria, perhaps speaking another language, that not only is he utterly familiar with contemporary British culture, he also writes in a clear and sometimes poetic English style about this important topic. I would recommend this book to any Christian, Catholic or Protestant, who wishes to enjoy a more intimate walk with Jesus whose love is poured into our hearts by the Holy Spirit (cf. Rm 5:5).

Pat Collins CM
Author, *Intimacy, and the Hungers of the Heart*

Chapter One

TREASURE OF THE HEART

Introduction

Jesus said to his disciples: "Do not store up for yourselves treasures on earth, where moth and decay destroy, and thieves break in and steal. But store up treasures in heaven, where neither moth nor decay destroys, nor thieves break in and steal. For where your treasure is, there also will your heart be" (Matthew 6:19-21).

The Scriptures have always, and rightly so, presented heaven as priceless, something beyond what humanity has ever known. It is a treasure that pulls the heart onward in the hope of its attainment. Thus, St. Paul says, *"No eye has seen, no ear has heard, no heart has imagined, what God has prepared for those who love Him."*

If you played treasure hunt games as a child, you might remember these key features of the hunted treasures: they were often hidden, priceless, and difficult to attain. But more importantly, the search for the treasure dictated the whole game. The settings, the moves you made, and even the way you felt were directly or indirectly influenced by the hunted treasure. You didn't even count the things you lost in the process. As children, we would often become oblivious to time and would have to be reminded that it was time to eat. The game on its own was interesting but would have meant very little without the treasure around which it was designed. Driven by this desire to find these hidden gems, I would restart the game as soon as it ended, constantly aiming for the treasure.

Now this is simply a children's game as I remember it. But isn't life a game in some sense, except that it is real and no joke? Isn't it true that some rules and treasures or *"telos"* dictate the direction of our lives? In this sense, therefore, life could be seen as a treasure-driven journey, hence, it is by no means purposeless. Life is purposeful in itself since it is gifted for a purpose that becomes its drive and indeed its utmost treasure.

It must be said here though, that Matthew 6:19-21 is not intending to suggest that the earth and its treasures should be despised or that one should be hesitant about pursuing those things which are perceived as treasures by the human heart. To do that would contradict the very nature of the human person created, who has been commanded to be fruitful and increase here on earth. It follows then that the earth itself should be treasured by human beings since it is a precious gift for which we must take responsibility as stewards. Of the earth, the Lord says, till, cultivate and tend it.

The human being is necessarily caught in a peculiar triangular relationship between self, God and the rest of the created order. These three: the person, God and the created order (which includes our neighbour) must be valued, treasured and held dear and very close to one's heart, to truly flourish and attain true happiness. The peace and abiding sense of well-being a person enjoys depends on the degree to which they can keep in balance the dynamism of this relationship. One attains this balance by treasuring each party appropriately, justly, and giving no more and no less than what is due.

The relationship is true for every individual, believer or non-believer since not even the latter can claim to be devoid of a sense of ultimate goodness that is impressed on the person and immediately demands adherence. This is true because the claim not to believe in God throws the person into that moral process where they need to find a justifiable reason for their position and actions forthwith, that is if their actions and thoughts are not to be arbitrary both to themselves and to the created order with which they must maintain a relationship to truly flourish and be happy. As soon as one consciously or unconsciously begins to search for these moral foundations, the person reaches beyond himself or herself. It then follows that the eventual success in this unavoidable venture witnesses to the truth that we are subject to certain principles, laws, meanings and purposes that demand obedience.

Again, we return to a similar triangular relationship between the moral subject, the created order and these truths, purpose, meaning, or principle and their source, which demands obedience. The non-believer must then treasure these three to a degree appropriate to each. However, this truth or purpose or meaning upon which one's actions are based must be true and consistent with the created order as a whole and with our very nature as humans.

What the heart treasures

Most of us Christians are seldom conscious enough to periodically ask ourselves what our treasures are and where they lie. While it is very important to know what and where our treasures are, it is even more important to know what and where they should be. Treasure is like a lens through which the heart sees and weighs the world and the value of the things it contains, and then relates with them as appropriate. Like a paddle, the treasure of the heart steers one's life forward or backwards and can also stall it or even capsize it. Although the paddle may be very small compared to the boat, when the right paddle is rightly used, a big boat can be steered to the desired destination. Even more so is the treasure of the heart.

"Finally, beloved, whatever is true, whatever is honourable, whatever is just, whatever is pure,

whatever is pleasing, whatever is commendable, if there is any excellence and if there is anything worthy of praise, think about these things" (Philippians 4). St. Paul encourages the Christian to feed the heart and the mind with positives so that the heart can be trained to rejoice in and desire that which is good, honourable, pleasing, etc. The Apostle understood that life's direction and movement are determined by what the heart treasures, hence his invitation to engage in what could be called a spiritual exercise of choosing good as the object of our thoughts and heart's desire. I would say that this isn't the end yet. It is only part of the process of discovering one's true treasure. When there is a conscious or deliberate effort to supply the mind and heart with healthy thoughts, in a sense, the person becomes attentive enough to hear and know where their true treasure lies and that is the fundamental drive where all peripherals are removed.

The Christian whose heart's treasure is rightly known and placed, is more stable, collected and grounded in his ways. Hence, it is often said that the spiritual battlefield is the heart. What is not easily appreciated by many is the nature of this battle and what is targeted in the battle. In the spiritual battle of the heart, the first target is what the heart treasures, either to corrupt it or to wrongly reposition it to take control of the whole being. *"For where your treasure is, there will your heart be also."*[1] And I dare say also, that where your treasure is, there will your whole being be eventually. By implication then, whoever has the treasures controls or directs the "gate" because it is the nature of the human heart to be drawn to and directed by where its treasures lie. For its treasure, the heart sacrifices other things considered of less value. Our heart's treasure could also determine the values we place on other things which indeed must serve it. The Gospels talked about how, for the treasures of heaven, a believer now sells all possessions and even gives the money away just to keep and secure that which the heart has come to treasure.[2]

Is it not surprising how oblivious most of us can be about what is truly the ultimate treasure of our hearts? I am not talking about what we would want to be our treasure or what should be our heart's treasure. It is so easy to confuse what ought to be as what is. When you ask people to tell you

---
[1] Matt. 6:21
[2] Lk 12:33

what they treasure, they are most likely to give idealistic answers based on what they perceive to be culturally, religiously or secularly acceptable. For instance, in response to this question, the Christian is most likely to say that heaven is the true treasure of their heart and this could well be true for the person. However, to know one's true treasure requires careful and honest consideration. Only with honesty, humility and intentionality can we discover, sometimes with shock and surprise, what truly is our deep-seated drive, our true treasure.

By divine design, the treasure of the heart, more often than not, needs to be *discovered* as it is seldom immediately accessible to us. There is a similarity between the discovery of the true treasure of one's heart and the biblical story of the discovery of the kingdom. The Scripture described the kingdom as a treasure hidden in a field. When a man found it, *"he hid it again, and in his joy, he went and sold all he had and bought that field."*[3]

Now, here is the thing. The true treasure of the heart, once discovered, directs the heart and the whole being. It becomes the principles upon

---
[3] Matt. 13:44

which moral decisions are made. Because of its value, one guards it with everything he or she has. As St. Matthew tells us, *"When he found it, he hid it again,"* not wanting to risk it being found by another. The man went off to sell everything he had to buy the land. His whole life became about the treasure. What the reader could easily miss in this parable is this: from that moment, all he had was that treasure for which he had given all to have. The discovery of one's true heart's treasure is indeed life-changing.

True treasure: a fire within

When I was discussing this topic with a priest friend of mine, he told me about something he had read, something about the importance of getting our treasure right. He spoke of a writer that used the analogy of the relationship between an addict and his or her addiction. The writer says, "You don't ask a drug addict where his treasure lies…as it is obvious that all he wants is the drug. He is directed and conditioned by it." It must be immediately said here that this is a very inaccurate analogy since addiction is one of those extreme situations where the will is dangerously weakened and hijacked from the moral subject in such a way that taking drugs cannot rightly be called his or her decision. In fact, to a drug addict, one may even argue that drugs can no longer be called treasure since the victim would most often wish not to take it but unfortunately remains incapable of stopping. Nonetheless, this analogy depicts a wrong treasure and its power to consume. However, the true and right treasure does not hijack our will, rather it powerfully impels it or urges it, not by a ruthless compulsion but by a consuming love which seduces infinitely and yet leaves the person with the will and choice.

"O Lord, you have seduced me, and I have allowed myself to be seduced."[4] This was Jeremiah's outcry as he contemplated his relationship with God. He couldn't explain how his love for God got him so steeped in suffering, yet he didn't resist. Hence, he said, *"And I allowed myself to be seduced."* Further on, in verse 9 of that chapter, Jeremiah exercises his will and decides not to preach about God anymore since this has brought him pain and mockery. But then this is what we hear, *"If I say, 'I will not mention him or speak any more in his name,'*

---
[4] Jer. 20:7

his message becomes a fire burning in my heart, shut up in my bones, and I become weary of holding it in, and I cannot prevail." [5] Now, the overpowering nature of this fire within him is nothing like the experience of the drug addict. Firstly, the fire within Jeremiah was a fire for good, to preach for the salvation of others and his own. This can't be said of drug addiction. Secondly, unlike the drug addict, Jeremiah isn't a victim of evil but a captive of true love. Thirdly, what was before Jeremiah to resist was good, while the person with substance misuse problems has to resist evil. Fourth, in the end, Jeremiah experiences true peace, with no guilt for yielding to his true desire. On the contrary, a drug addict is left in guilt and wounded for yielding to the wrong destructive treasure that now preys on him or her. However, one of the many things that are common in both experiences is the fact that they both were overpowered by their hearts' treasures, albeit for different purposes.

What you truly treasure often directs your path. Do not waste your precious time trying to change your ways if you haven't yet considered the driving force that has brought you to that path,

---
[5] Jer. 20:9

else after having invested so much effort in walking in a desired path, if ever that would be possible, you still end up in the undesired path. What is at play is the heart's true desires. Find your heart's true treasure, work on it prayerfully and honestly and you will achieve the right direction in your life.

Impelled by attraction

If life were a dance, the treasure of the heart would dictate the tune. Therefore, whoever dictates the tune, controls or conditions the dancing style. While this is not a very good analogy, it offers some idea as to how subtle and yet powerful the treasure of the heart can be.

If you want your child or the faithful entrusted to you to flourish very well in life, start early to inculcate in them what they should treasure most. Through your living example, let them see the beauty of it. It will take time to grow and to take a foundational place where it becomes a context within which every other action is based. If you succeed in helping your children choose the ultimate treasure (which is God), then you have done them the ultimate good which summons obedience from all other desires. This is indeed the true *telos* which all human desire seeks to attain (unfortunately, often through the wrong means). Here, I do not mean the desire to enter into a relationship with God and do his will simply as a moral obligation. I mean a true beauty that unconsciously calls out from the beholder a sense of wonder, drawing in and eventually overwhelming the person. Unlike a drug addict who falls into the captivity of addiction, this one witnesses an impelling and invading beauty that draws them to freedom, purpose and fruitfulness, empowering them to freely give up will and self, whilst still retaining the power to take it back. *"I lay down my life to take it up again. No one takes it from me; I lay it down of my own free will. And as it is in my power to lay it down, so it is in my power to take it up again. And this is the command I have been given by my Father."*[6]

Jesus' love and faithfulness to his Father's will, besides Him being fully God and Man, is a response to love. He was impelled by love. Even though He referred to the laying down of His life as a command, we must understand it as a radical

---

[6] Jn. 10:17-18

response to the impelling power of love and beauty experienced in the Father with whom He is one. In this way, He freely set aside His own will and chose the Father, in whom He had placed all He was and had. With Jesus, we see how His heart's treasure propelled Him to yield to the Father's love. Indeed, this is holiness.

Chapter Two

LOVE IN OUR HEARTS AS A DRIVE FOR HOLINESS

Love in our hearts

Those who have experienced love or, to use the common expression, falling in love, may have noticed that what I have been describing as the treasure of the heart is, in fact, equivalent to the nature of love. Love impels, does it not? For the beloved, the lover makes sacrifices, and in a perfect scenario, lives for her/him who has become a treasure for the lover. We see this in the love of parents towards their children. Because of their love towards their children, they go out of their way to care for, keep and protect them.

Do not underestimate the power of love, its power to hold the one who has fallen for it captive. I had a friend whom I trusted so much, and I asked him to do something for me—I paid him, of course. Unfortunately, he didn't do it as I had instructed, but he lied about having done it. He had used part of the money to feed his children who were starving. When I found out, I was cross and felt betrayed by this particular friend. I called him to talk about it, and he apologised but made excuses, which got me even more upset. It made me decide never to entrust him with any job again. Then one day, in a conversation about that same issue, he said something like, "I couldn't watch my family starve." That struck me.

Now, do not get what I am about to say wrong; I am not justifying lies and deceit, no. What my friend did was wrong and remains wrong. He could have asked me for help. I don't remember refusing him any help before so long as it was something I could assist him with. However, reflecting on why he betrayed his life-long friend, I could not help seeing that he had to do what he did for the love he had for his family. Ordinarily, my friend would never have betrayed me. But his love for his children whom he treasured so much, drove him to ignore the imminent consequence of his actions, even though he could have satisfied the same demand through other justifiable (albeit more difficult) means, without having to betray himself, his friend and indeed God. While this could be seen as a misguided way to act about a genuine feeling of love, it nonetheless shows how the treasure of the heart could almost uncontrollably direct the whole being. This is why Song of Songs 8:7 says, *"Love is something that no flood can quench, no torrents drown. Were a man to offer all the wealth of his house to buy love, contempt is all he would purchase."*

Love as knowledge

Like love, the treasure of the heart is stronger than the torrents and floods of life. To the heart, its true treasure seems to dwarf the value of all everything around, causing it to look upon it with somewhat contempt when compared to its desire. Thus, St. Paul, in his letter to the Philippians (chapter 3), gives a good picture of this reality. He realises that, compared to the supreme knowledge of Christ all things become dispensable. Thus, St Paul said, *"I believe that nothing can happen that will outweigh the supreme advantage of knowing Christ Jesus my Lord. For him, I have accepted the loss of everything, and I look at everything as so much rubbish if only I can have Christ and be given a place in him."* [7]

So, for the sake of what St. Paul had discovered in Christ (or came to treasure), truth or knowledge he qualified as supreme, every other thing in his life began to take its rightful place. That which was offered in Christ became the first and guiding principle and consequently becoming the scale of measurement for other things. The power of this *gift* in Christ had given him so much freedom that he could look upon other things and freely give them up. For what? So that he might retain that which is offered in Christ. Doesn't this remind us of the parable of the kingdom of heaven that we discussed earlier? Jesus tells us that it is like a treasure someone finds, hides, and then goes home, selling all he has so that he may have it. Like St. Paul, we are to guard and treasure this gift of God in Christ above all else.

---
[7] Phil. 3:8-14

Examination: The way to guard the heart

The treasure of our heart controls, or rather, informs the rules of the many games of life and determines the value of each game. So, what I intend to do here is to propose some things that one might do to guard the heart to treasure rightly. First, carefully and doggedly discern to know what your deepest and ultimate heart's treasure is; test this discovery in the light of your present lifestyle to find out its authenticity. Secondly, get it right because your future is more or less a product of your heart's ultimate treasure. Once that is done, constantly be awake and spiritually sensitive to know when you are shifting or being led away from it. As I said, this is where the spiritual battle mostly resides. Hence, the Bible says, *"More than all else, keep watch over your heart, since here are the wellsprings of life."* [8] Some translations would say, guard your heart with all diligence. Whilst a security guard ought to keep an eye on every area he has been entrusted to guard, he or she focuses more on the most important places, where security is most likely to be compromised. The same applies to us as the chief

---
[8] Prov. 4:23

safe guarders of our hearts' gate. We must concern ourselves with the most decisive place in the spiritual battle or confrontation, and that is the treasure of our heart, constantly reviewing it to ensure that it is still what it should be and is rightly positioned.

The heart's treasure and the Christian life of holiness

I do think that the core idea behind the examination of conscience isn't so much about sin and guilt, although those could surface later in the process. It is principally about what we have been dealing with here, the treasure of the heart. When we closely examine our actions, they offer a lens or a mirror through which we understand the state of our heart and what it truly treasures. We can then reinforce or reconsider the treasure, whatever it may be. The treasure of the heart bears fruits in one's actions. Thus, our actions are consistent with what we treasure. One cannot treasure base things and then expect to soar high in life and attain true happiness and fulfilment. True fulfilment can only be accessed through the gates of the heart when it is sincerely and humbly examined and listened to.

"If then you have been raised with Christ, seek the things that are above, where Christ is seated at the right hand of God. Set your minds on things that are above, not on things that are on earth." [9] With these words, St. Paul instructs the young Christian Community in Colossi on how to live free from what he called "the elemental spirit of the universe" so that no one might delude them and make prey of them. [10] Apostle Paul offers what could be considered a remedy to the deceptive wiles of the enemy of our salvation, and that is getting right one's heart's treasure. St. Paul invited the Colossians to rise above the base to treasure that which lies above, that which endures. In St. Paul's thoughts, we can live a true Christian life only to the extent to which we can set as our hearts' treasure that which endures and lies above us, that which cannot be touched by the vicissitudes of the passing world. Only then do we stand the chance of putting to death what he calls the earthly in us - *"fornication, impurity, passion, evil desire, covetousness which is idolatry, anger, malice, wrath, slander, lies, etc."* —and strive to attain *"compassion, kindness, lowliness, meekness and patience."*[11]

---
[9] Col. 3:1-2
[10] Col. 2:4,8,20
[11] Col. 3:5-7, 12

If Christian obedience is a response to love, then one could say that Christian obedience is driven by the treasure of the heart. For what a heart truly loves, it treasures, delights in and obeys.

The Lord, our Treasure

Often, we attempt the impossible in our Christian living because we undertake what I have termed a fruitless endeavour of trying to climb a tree from the top. When the treasure is not rightly considered, we often pray amiss. We do not receive what we ask for because we pray with the wrong kind of motive. What then would help us get our motives right, regardless of how pious and religious they might appear to us? It is the true treasure of one's heart. Spend more time in prayers to discern what yours truly is, and not what you want it to be or what you think it should be. Once you start engaging in this exciting and often astonishing adventure, the content of your prayer begins to take shape and gets rightly directed. It doesn't matter what the outcome is. What matters is that you are sincerely discerning. If you discover that all the while you have been driven by the wrong desire, do not worry, and do not be disillusioned because the discovery itself is huge progress. The awareness of one's state will always be better than the contrary. When one realises by grace that the true heart treasure has been wrongly placed, then such a person is most likely going to retrace their steps, reposition and pray for a revival or a renewal. As I suggested earlier, carefully discern your actions. I say this because they offer us a mirror which shows us where our heart's treasure truly lies.

Take for example, how you behave in a conversation or discourse. Do you always want to control, dominate and have your way in every situation? If yes, the next question to answer carefully is "Why is that the case?" It might be that you simply can't deal with not being at the centre of attention. Still, this requires further careful discernment. Why am I always obsessive about being at the centre of attention? Could it be because I feel rewarded by it? But why do I feel rewarded by it? You can go on until you either do not know the answer anymore or discover the vanity of your constant desire to dominate and control. You might also discover that it flows from a sense of lack of true meaning which can only come from that which lies above us. If one's heart treasure lies in what is base, it leaves the Christian often craving for meaning and purpose. When this is not found within oneself, there is a reaching out to others, not for self-giving but to take from them and use them, hence the craving to dominate and control. Yet, all this is a search for that which lies beyond the person.

However, the Christian whose treasure is truly that which transcends all things will find a meaning that surpasses what the world could ever offer. Therefore, prompted and guided by the heart's treasure, one reaches out to others not to dominate or control but does so for mutual nourishment, and, when needed, for self-giving. A heart whose treasure is the Lord delights in Him. Its motive is directed rightly, what the heart truly desires is found in and flows from God. Indeed, this reality is the very nature of the human person, hence the psalmist rightly says, *"Take delight in the Lord, and he will give you the desires of your hearts."* However, it must be said here that this truth is understood only in the sense that the delight (treasure) of the heart informs the desire. It presupposes that the latter (the desire which is to be granted) is born of the former (one's true treasure which is God). Hence, it is without doubt that the latter will be granted, but only when they have been informed by and tend towards the true delight of the heart, which in this case is God. That said, we must also bear in mind that not all desires we perceive as good or even pious and religious, are born of this delight in God, who is the ultimate treasure.

Another illustration would be when a Christian says that his or her true treasure is to do the will of God. As religious and pious as this might sound, the Christian, through careful and prayerful examination, must continuously discern to ensure that this continues to be true. A sincere and careful discernment might raise the question of why. Why do I treasure the will of God and how far can I go in sticking to this will? Am I willing to stick to it even at the cost of everything? The Christian discerns deeper to know what that treasure is for which he or she is willing to suffer the loss of all things. *"For we have left everything to follow you. What then shall we have?"*[12]

One's true treasure is to the heart a sufficient reward for which all things could be endured, lost or sacrificed. In the end, the Christian may

---
[12] Matt. 19:27

discover that it is only for him or herself that he or she is willing to lose all things, in which case, with humility and sincerity, the Christian's discernment has borne the good fruit of knowing where his heart truly lies. But one should then, by grace, prayer and other spiritual exercises, train the heart to desire rightly.

When we move against the tide

Let us return to the Christian response that claims that doing God's will is one's heart's treasure. The crucial question to ask in discerning the truthfulness of this claim is, would one wish to stick to God's will till the end, even when it is considered wrong and sinful by everyone? Would one stick to God's will even when it brings shame and disrepute to society? What if doing God's will demands not doing that which one truly believed to be religious and pious? Would one still delight in and treasure God's will if it launched him or her into an uncertain and dark territory?

"Even though I walk through the valley of the shadow of death, I fear no evil. Though an army encamps around me, my heart will not fear; though a war breaks out against me, I will keep my trust… One thing I have

asked of the LORD; this is what I desire: to dwell in the house of the LORD all the days of my life, to gaze on the beauty of the LORD and seek Him in His temple." [13] I suppose only one's true treasure of the heart can sustain one in a time of uncertainty. But then if our heart's treasure is feeble, and can easily be weakened or touched by the tyranny of the elemental spirit of the universe, we may not stand a chance of overcoming at last. Even if we present God as our true treasure, in the end, our lives will mirror not only to us but to the world what our true heart treasure is, whether it be earthly or none other than God.

Getting the treasure of the heart right and rightly placed takes primacy in Christian living. Choose the ultimate treasure, reinforce it, and you will attain the greatest height. You are worth the life of God since your salvation cost the life of God. Therefore, make no mistake of allowing things that are not worth your life to be the lens through which you view the world. Do not let things lower than you be the driving force of your whole being. Pick the right treasure, nurture your heart to love and delight in it, and then see that the outcome of

---
[13] Ps 23:4, Ps 27:3,4

your life will depend on what your heart truly treasures.

Chapter Three

IMPLICATIONS OF THE IMITATION OF CHRIST

Jesus' self-emptying: Implications

At the heart of the reasons for writing this book is simply a quest to re-contemplate what helps the Christian to walk faithfully in God's will — a place where our safety and peace lie. In everything I have been saying so far, what is actually at stake is the salvation of one's soul. What the heart treasures plays a central role in a Christian's obedient submission to the Lord, without which we risk losing the salvation of our souls. As always, we can look at Jesus and learn from what He did and thought. *"Learn from me for I am gentle and humble in heart."*[14] *"Let this mind be in you which was also in Christ Jesus."*[15]

The fundamental truth about Jesus' kenosis is that of a complete self-emptying of the treasures of His heart into His Father's hands. *"His state was divine, yet he did not cling to his equality with God but emptied himself."*[16] Having emptied everything He was into His Father's hands, it then follows that His will, passions, heart and indeed His whole life were directed and affixed to that place where His treasures were. Jesus chose the Father's will over His own, and it became all that mattered to Him.[17] As such, His thoughts, actions and words were all guided by His treasure, which is the Father and His will. Having loved us so much as His treasures, He again offered us to His Father.[18] The whole of Jesus's life was very kenotic. This finally culminated in His complete self-offering on the cross. Jesus did not only give all He treasured — His equality with God and the glory of His majesty, us, His children whom He loved eternally — He also gave His own life on the cross.

---

[14] *Matt. 11:29*
[15] Phil 2:5
[16] Phil 2:6-7a
[17] John 4:34
[18] John 17:9-10

The former could rightly be seen as a result of His heart and will, which, eternally, are being steered by the treasures of His heart, namely His love for His father's will and His love for us. The Scripture hints at this when it grants us access to the driving force behind Jesus' endurance and perseverance till the end. It says, *"Let us fix our eyes on Jesus, the author and perfector of our faith, who for the joy set before him endured the cross, scorning its shame, and sat down at the right hand of the throne of God."*[19]

I suppose the question here is, what joy was set before Him? Let's immediately make it clear that the joy set before Jesus transcends simply sitting at the right hand of the throne of God, for this has always been his rightful place' It is who He is by nature; thus it is not something new. Therefore, this joy set before Him is more about seeing the fulfilment of the will of His father, for which He had stripped Himself of all things, and the will to save us whom He loved in eternity and for whom He will become an eternal high priest, making an unfailing intercession.

---

[19] Hebrews 12:2

Freedom from oppression

Jesus' invitation for us to set aright the treasure of our hearts does not only have future implications. Some might be tempted to suggest that it has only to do with eternal blessedness or the fullness of salvation. We can see in some sense that Jesus wants us to understand, first and foremost, its implication in the now before the future. The latter part of that invitation as it were brings out its motive. *"For where your treasure is, there also will your heart be"* (Matthew 6:19-21). The heart is steered by the locus of its treasure.

Most times, deliverance from demonic influences is really about a re-direction or retrieval of the treasure of the heart, so that hearts held bound by the negative influence and the consequence of the misplacements of the heart's treasures, could be freed. Some are today besieged by a spirit of misery, sadness, and lack of peace, even when they have most things that life can offer. We hear people say things like, 'I am a sad person, and I do not know why I am this sad. I wish I could be a little happy in my life." More often than not, this is oppression by the evil one. When one is endemically consumed with sadness, strength wastes away (Nehemiah 8:10), and very quickly, peace vanishes. Thus, a victorious Christian living becomes impossible at that moment. Jesus came to give us joy and peace in a way that the world cannot give, so that, even amidst calamities and sufferings, we can still experience a depth of peace and joy that flows from the source unto which our hearts are drawn, since in Him we have heaped all our treasures. Therefore, we are strengthened to stand the waves and tides of life in a very miraculous and inexplicable way because the heart has invested itself firmly in the Word, which is our rock.

The Gospel of Matthew 7:24-27, describes one whose heart's treasure is the Lord as one who has built his house on the rock. Rain and wind came against the house, yet it did not fall. Why? It had its foundation on the rock. To build on the rock as the Gospel explains is about investing one's life in the Word, the rock which then becomes one's firm foundation. A house built on that foundation, which is Jesus the truth, is most founded to withstand the fiery snares of the enemy.

The lure

Sometimes, souls are lured and not forced into captivity, so that with their own free choice, though ignorantly, they consent and walk into captivity by their lifestyle. Christian freedom is lost as one gradually places more value on things one shouldn't. A typical example would be when a Christian begins to spend more time on unfruitful things than they would invest in something fruitful or productive. Prayer time slowly starts to be burdensome. Things of God now become things we that are rushed through to spend time on other things. When prayer life weakens, Christians become spiritually weak, even though they may still appear before people as being sound and spiritual. Within this foundation, subtle addictions begin to creep into one's life. Since the spiritual alertness is tuned down, the sense of sin begins to weaken. This may continue until there is no more fear and dread of the deep valley of sin and its hydra-headed character. We make excuses for our sins. We could even go as far as finding pastors, theological books and friends that patronise us and our state.

Weighed down by the heaviness of their captivity, our hearts are no longer able to treasure above all else that which is set above. Therefore, they crave the material and passing things of this world, which, in most cases, would still have been given when the heart treasures God above all else, even above one's self. Since the true heart's treasure can never be found in the base things of this world, the heart is lured into a maze of captivity where it is lost spiritually, seeking in the world that which it must find only by looking beyond the created order. As a consequence, instead of being able to use the good things of this world in a way that looks forward to that which is eternal, we fall captive to what we should exercise control over.

The gift of the body and all its emotions and dimensions, rather than becoming gifts which we constantly offer to God as sweet-smelling offerings (Romans 12:1-2), now become objects of sinfulness and sensual inventiveness. At this point, we cannot help ourselves anymore. We actually need salvation from ourselves. Having displaced God from His place as the principal desire of the human heart, we are no longer able to use His gifts as instruments of salvation. Rather, we turn them against ourselves and, consequently, against God.

Even though this spiritual battle is in the realm of

the human mind, in recent times, it is becoming increasingly aggressive. We are bombarded with tons of thoughts, images and information. You don't necessarily have to go searching for them before they come to you. Some, without knowing, have been absorbed into tides of destructive ideas and thoughts which have caused them to be spiritually sedated in their sins. It is no longer news how traumatised our young people are today. Most (adults included) have been lured to abandon faith and the search for truth that transcends mere personal preferences. As a result, many have ended up confused, frustrated and lacking the joy and peace that faith offers. They set out searching for the ultimate treasure within the passing things of this world, where it certainly can never be found. Disappointed and pained by the increasing lack of meaning, they consider taking their own lives. Listen, I am in no way saying that people with faith do not go through difficult times or even consider suicide. I am saying that a believer whose heart's treasure is indeed God, is more likely to anchor their life on something that triumphs over the vicissitudes of the passing world. Faith grants access to that which transcends the person and which now becomes a strong and unfailing life anchor.

When I was a chaplain to a homelessness charity here in London, I had the privilege of having a homeless person share with me how their faith kept them going through a traumatising experience. I clearly remember one saying during our prayer meetings that she had often wondered how the homeless, who are in a very terrible situation, could find meaning and believe that tomorrow would be better. It is not as if they do not have a choice of killing themselves, no. "But we are inexplicably hopeful, a hope that is often inaccessible to many who, despite their riches, commit suicide in the comfort of their homes." When she said this, I thought that was very profound.

What we try to explore here is what really drives the heart and gives it a sense of purpose, direction, strength and meaning. This is what I have called the treasure of the heart. One's heart's desire could also be argued to be the sustainer of one's hope. Thus the Scripture says that *"for the joy set before him, Jesus endured the cross, despising the shame, and is seated at the right hand of the throne of God"* (Hebrews 12:2). The hope that was set before Jesus was the joy. This joy empowered and attracted Him upward, overcoming shame and the cross.

Even so, our hearts' treasures empower us, especially in the face of the scandals and the contradictions that our faith often throws us into. This is very important if our hearts must walk the narrow path of truth and attain its destined glorious future. What the heart treasures must be strong enough to transcend and overcome the stumbling blocks we must confront in faithfulness and patience. In the next chapter, we shall look at the scandals, contradictions and paradoxes of the faith which the Christian's heart's treasure must be strong enough to face, and which God alone can be a strong-enough treasure to overcome.

Chapter Four

THE CHRISTIAN FAITH AS A SCANDAL OF PERFECT LOVE

Living the scandal of the cross

The Christian faith has always been and will remain a scandal to a world that has lost its way from the vision of the creator who loves it so much and offered His son for its redemption. The centrality of the cross makes this truth even more dazzling. It is the truth that the cross, which was an instrument of torture, shame and curse, has now in Christ's death, become the wood upon which hangs the salvation of the world, the wood upon which the tree of life is restored to the lost humanity. This will remain incomprehensible, perhaps eternally. That the King of kings reigned from the cross and manifested from there His power in the most vulnerable state (of being humiliated, battered, bruised and pierced) to the world can be considered anything but definitely not power and strength as we know it in our world. How could power and strength be manifested in weakness and vulnerability?

To imagine that the Christian God died for the creatures and still lives is absolute foolishness to the human reason. The creation accounts of many religions presenting gods as the served, and the creatures simply dispensable and there to serve the gods. The creatures reach towards the gods to appease them lest they be struck. They constantly offer sacrifices to quench the hunger and thirst of the gods. But in the Christian God, made manifest in Jesus, all of that turned. God comes, serves human beings, dies for them, and gives them the water of life to quench their thirst. Yet, He remains God, the all-powerful and the immortal. This truth amazes even the Christian, and the belief in it is enabled only by the supernatural gift of faith. How then do we expect the world to understand us without the penetration of the divine light of salvation?

I am sorry to bring this "bad news" to you. Just as

Christ's life remained a scandal till today, so does our authentic Christian life remain a scandal for many and a cause of confusion to the wise and the strong. The Christian's duty is not to make the faith less scandalous but rather to faithfully live that tension, that scandal, so that the human reason will constantly be summoned to mount on the wings of faith to perceive the power of its truth. It is only through our faithfulness to this truth that the world stands the chance of believing. Any other option risks compromising the very core of the Christian faith and would strip it of its power to save. When this happens, the new convert comes in, and with a surprising disappointment finds nothing supernatural to encounter.

It might also surprise you to know that your true and profound Christian joy will depend on the acceptance of this truth. Only then can our lives exude the power of God's presence, which often flows from that place of tension, a place where this scandal meets our faithfulness and total abandonment. This is the power behind the Resurrection. Jesus did not overcome death by fighting and resisting it. Christ's victory lies precisely in His total abandonment to the power of death and in His obedience to the Father's will.

Through this encounter (between Jesus' faithful abandonment and the vindictive power of death), which Balthazar called "descent into hell," death is overpowered and destroyed and the Resurrection and life are revealed. For a Christian to live a victorious resurrection life, he or she must learn to abandon himself or herself and live amidst that scandal, so that through us, the darkness and cloud of unbelief cast over people's minds by ignorance and pride might be dispelled by the light of faith.

Pride resists this path of living the scandal of our faith. It often appears compassionate to the people who are scandalised by the faith, but in the end produces people in the Church who do not really believe in the core of the faith, perhaps through no fault of their own. As a result, our Church risks becoming a social construct bereft of the supernatural life in the Spirit, which can only be lived in the embracing of this scandal.

Why am I saying this? It is to encourage us when we find out that our faithfulness or truthfulness seems to scandalise others. Do not be surprised when people do not understand you on account of your faith founded in and expressed through charity. The reason is simple: your Lord and

Master was and is a scandal. The truth you bear witness to distresses many. Even the life you are living gracefully can upset a lot of people. When that happens, do not try to escape the scandal. Be ready to offer an explanation (1 Peter) in word and deed but always impelled by love.

If the Christian is Christ-like, then our lives are like that of Jesus in the bread of life discourse in John 6. There Jesus told the people that He is the true bread from heaven that one eats and never dies. The people resisted and couldn't take it. Jesus, in love, persisted and even went deeper to say that one must eat His flesh and drink His blood to have eternal life. Was Jesus insensitive? We cannot possibly imagine that. Was He deriving joy in their confusion? Jesus, being the incarnate divine love, could not have done that. So, what was happening there? Jesus knew quite well how confusing and even provoking those words must have been. But the truth is that there was no other way to present that central truth without risking adulteration. Patiently, Jesus remained and endured, loving them even in their unbelief. They were the ones who walked away, and even then, Jesus couldn't swerve from the truth to get rid of the scandal and keep them.

This does not mean that we don't approach people where they are as we try to witness to God's love, no. But we do not change the truth. There could always be a gradual progression to exposing one to the truth of faith, but this process does not involve tempering with the truth in order to make it more acceptable. A delay in the journey of discovering the self-revealing truth could be dealt with by taking certain areas of the topic in a timely manner and addressing them, while remaining faithful to the truth. To be able to do this, what is required is a prayerful, humble and patient approach. We remain with the people, loving them even in their unbelief and faithfully offering possible explications of the truth.

The prideful is not patient in this process. Hence, he or she quickly changes the truth under the pretext of being compassionate, an act which is often a sign of a hidden inability to remain and live that rigour of the faith and endure the embarrassment and shame whilst waiting for a divine passage to be granted. Naturally, this is our first instinct: to get rid of these tensions and scandals that come on account of our faith. However, the divine invitation is to remain and embrace it with patient trust and openness to the one who speaks through all things.

Human life is lived within the reality of this contradiction

Life is good and beautiful. Life is precious. As much as these adjectives are very true of human life, they are experienced only within deep-seated contradictions and scandals. Life is beautiful and yet filled with ugliness, pain, suffering and the eventual reality of passing away. We live with the knowledge of that which is young now will get old, that which is strong now will get weak, that which we live for and labour for we must, in time, leave behind. We plan, always aware that our plans aren't the blueprint. We are not in control, and every control we have attained as humans always leads to other uncontrollable problems.

We are changed by every moment. We rejoice in the reality of this change because it means that our pains are transient. For indeed, weeping may last for the night, but joy comes in the morning. Yet the reality of this change also means that we are not exactly the same as we were seconds ago. As beautiful as our present might be, it is not ours to keep. Time reminds and teaches us that truth. In the end, life is not without purpose. But its purpose is lived within a full range of contradictions.

Amid these contradictions, we are called to insist on and defend the truth that life is beautiful and worth living. Unfortunately, sometimes we have to defend the beauty of life before people whose poverty is the source of riches for others. How could we, before the abused and the enslaved, still insist on this preciousness and beauty of life? In a world known to thrive in the unfortunate adage, "Might is right," a place where the strong exploit the weak and claim it is a favour, a world where millions are dying of hunger while trillions are spent on the invention of nuclear warheads, a world where some have been made to believe that their lives are less important than others.' This is the world where we are to witness the beauty of life. How easy and convenient could that possibly be?

How can we bear witness to this objective truth of the beauty of human life without feeling the force of these contradictions, without feeling like we are mocking the people we witness? At this point, one could even begin to doubt one's own belief, one's own faith. These contradictions in our reality have caused many people to cower and withdraw from witnessing the beauty of life. Unfortunately, and dangerously too, many who defend the beauty of life do it oblivious to these contradictions. One cannot successfully witness the beauty of life outside the context of these contradictions. Ignoring it and coating it with some religious or pious jargon is a denial of the reality of the very nature and character of the life we live. It is only by living within these contradictions, striving to be true to ourselves, do we stand the chance of witnessing successfully to the beauty of human life amid its existential contradictions.

The wound is the invitation

When I was chaplain at the homelessness charity which I mentioned earlier, we usually took our clients on a trip once a month as a way of allowing them to share in the joys of life. Often, we would take them to places they would otherwise not have been and they liked it. On one of these trips, we visited Aylesford Priory, a place that is home to the Order of the Carmelites. That day happened to be a retreat day for the Legion of Mary, which also coincided with the Memorial of Our Lady of Fatima. There was a Holy Mass at the shrine, and we all went. We had our lunch after the Mass, rested, then set off to visit the Garden of Peace and the Rosary Way. After which we went up to a library. As you could imagine, it was full of books written by Carmelite saints. Knowing that the Carmelites are contemplatives, I decided to search for any book on the theme of sufferings.

While I was scanning through the shelves one of the ladies in the group asked what I was looking for. At first, I was hesitant about telling her, suspecting what her reaction would be. But after a while, I replied, "Books on sufferings."

I could see shock on her face as she asked, "Sufferings? Oh no! Sufferings?"

I said yes. And she pressed on. "Why?"

Before I could respond, she walked away. I followed her, explaining because I noticed she had become a bit uncomfortable.

The word suffering has become unbearable and evokes unpleasant emotions. It seems that today, the only way most people deal with suffering is to simply not talk about it or to simply deny it and pretend it doesn't exist. It is similar to the way we treat sin. The sad truth is that suffering is part of our existential condition. We live in and witness through and in it.

When I finally succeeded in persuading the lady to listen to me, I explained why I was looking for the book. I told her that a parishioner had mentioned something about suffering and wounds which made me want to read up more on that. After explaining all the whys, she seemed just a bit convinced. Anyway, we laughed over it. But here is the funny side. As I continued to scan through the shelves, I picked up a book at random and it was titled, *From Ashes to Fire*. I had to put it down immediately, thinking, "Hello? That is rather too much. From ashes to fire!" When I shared the experience with the ladies, they laughed. I could imagine them thinking, "You wanted to read about suffering? Here is the real stuff. Why are you running away?" In all this, you can see how we naturally avoid things that seem to complicate life. And yet life is not without its maze of complications.

Now here is the full context surrounding my search for the book on suffering and the eventual attempt to write this section on, "The wound is the invitation." The night before we went on that trip, during our parish prayer meeting, we talked about Christian witnessing. It was a Bible-sharing group where everyone was inivited to share their thoughts. We strived to allow the Word of God to be broken to us. In the course of our conversations, we raised the issues of the challenges to Christian witnessing. A young man gave what you could call an exhortation and testimony at the same time. He talked about his journey of faith and how the previous three years had been a momentous faith adventure and growth. He talked about how his experience of God's love makes it impossible not to witness it. In his words, "How dare I forget after all He had done?" I am not sure whether he was quoting someone else here. He went ahead and shared an experience he had when he wanted to write a publication about a charity he had set up with his partner and was asked to remove a phrase or so which referred to Christ.

"My partner and I talked about it," he said. "Knowing that Christ is the whole essence of the charity, removing him from the picture would defeat the whole purpose." So, with wisdom and perseverance, they insisted, and the work was published. The whole point of the testimony was to encourage others who might have been experiencing those subtle but vicious persecutions or aggressions against our faith or our other deep-seated convictions.

The courage that stems from love is needed to stay true to our convictions because, often we risk everything in doing so. When this young man and his partner insisted on mentioning Christ as being at the heart of their work, they risked everything. But God, who gives increase, granted them passage. Would that then be the end of these tensions? Definitely not. As long as they insist on remaining true to Christ as the centre of that charity, they must expect to live in that reality of their faithfulness, bringing them discomfort. But this is a good discomfort because, even then, they would have that peace that Christ gives (John 14:27). These contradictions are the sufferings we must bear on account of our faith. The experiences we go through in our resolve to stay faithful constitute the fire that purifies, heals, and makes us instruments of healing.

The prayer meeting had ended, and we were talking about how the meeting went, when the same parishioner said, "The wound is the invitation."

I immediately said "Yes, the wound is indeed the invitation." Our "woundedness," our scars and our sufferings are not without use. In fact, in them (which often result from our faith), lies a divine invitation to become channels of transcendent power.

"But we have this treasure in earthen vessels, to show that the transcendent power belongs to God and not to us. We are afflicted in every way, but not crushed; perplexed, but not driven to despair; persecuted, but not forsaken; struck down, but not destroyed, always carrying in the body the death of Jesus, so that the life of Jesus may also be manifested in our bodies" (2 Corinthians 4:7-10).

St. Paul tells the Christian community in Corinth the hard truth of the faith they had assented to. He makes it clear that the Christian life is lived in that tension between being healed and freed and being afflicted, between despair and having to hope, between the healing that Jesus' wounds make possible and having to carry upon our bodies the signs of Christ's sufferings. But all this is not without purpose. St. Paul tells us that it was *"so that the life of Jesus may be manifested in their bodies."* And if you think about it, what does the life of Jesus Christ do if not heal and restore us to fullness and abundance of life? Such are the lives of those who, through faithful and patient endurance, live in these contradictions and tensions, whose effects on human hearts could be seen as a form of suffering and being wounded. Our wounds therefore become an invitation to us and the world. They invite us not to denial but to acceptance, so that like Christ's, our wounds can become sources of encouragement and healing to others. In our wounds are the living experiences that speak more powerfully than mere theological or philosophical abstractions.

The fifty-third chapter of the book of the Prophet Isaiah (the suffering servant hymn) describes this. It starts with a rhetorical question that encapsulates the incredibility and the effects of the sufferings of God's servants. He says in verse one, *"Who has believed what we have heard? And to whom has the arm of the Lord been revealed?"* In verses three and four, the Prophet describes the terrible experience of the suffering servant and says, *"He was despised and rejected by men, a man of sorrows, acquainted with grief; and as one from whom men hide their faces he was despised, and we esteemed him not….he has borne our griefs and carried our sorrows."* In verse five, the Prophet flips to the other side of these sufferings — the effects, fruits and the healing they bear. He says, *"…and by his stripes we are healed."*

In Christ, our wounds are made sources of

healing. Hence, the Christian is invited, through careful discernment and prayer, to understand in what ways our own wounds, inadequacies, and sufferings could become sources of healing. Like Christ, whose wounds healed and who still heals us, we too become wounded healers when our contradictions and wounds are lived with courage. They witness to our faith more powerfully before people. Witnessing in these tensions that arise on account of our faith, is more powerful than presenting a façade of the Christian life as being all good.

His privileged choice of us

As mentioned earlier, the temptation is often to unduly focus on making our Christian faith presentable, acceptable and promising by hiding these uncomfortable wounds and scandals. But what this does is take away the realness, gives false hope and consequently takes away our faith. To engage with this Christian reality is to bear in mind the truth that if we were of the world, the world would love us as its own, in which case we may not have to deal with all this. However, being chosen by God has separated us from the world, in the sense that our way of life is in disparity with the ways and the thinking of our fallen world.

"If you were of the world, the world would love its own; but because you are not of this world, but I chose you out of the world, therefore the world hates you" (John 15:19).

Here, we immediately see the direct consequence of our privilege of being chosen by God, that is, a separation from the world whose enmity and rejection the Christian now suffers. This privileged path on which we walk, full of contradictions and paradoxes, is primarily a consequence of God's choice of us. His choice has put us here, on this narrow path. Our deliberate and conscious effort to accept and to walk in this path then becomes the fruits of our assent to this divine choice of us.

"If they (the world) hate you, remember that they hated me first" (John 15:20). Jesus' words here can often be very disturbing because they make us wonder how the peace He promised (John 14:27) could be experienced amidst all these troubles. Reading these words, the Christian immediately becomes aware that the Christian path of life would be anything but convenient. He or she is invited to enter into and engage with the fallen world and to

live in that constant encounter. Thus, Jesus says to us, "Just know that it is not unusual to your faithfulness to my choice of you."

Through the power of the Holy Spirit in us, we often see, perceive and hear things that the world in its fallen nature, unaided by faith, cannot see nor hear. However, this grace of perceiving as God perceives, also comes with pains and crosses. Often, where others, in ignorance, see peace, we could be seeing pain and injustice. On the other hand, when the world cries, "Trouble! Trouble!," we may see God walking upon the waters. Hence, we often groan in prayer, asking for divine help, like Jesus who, during his days on earth, offered up prayers and entreaties with loud cries to the One who could save Him (Hebrews 5:7). Being enlightened by the Holy Spirit, we live in shock as we see sin being normalised and the innocence of children taken as they are forced to learn things they shouldn't at their age. With the light of the Holy Spirit, the Christian sees how the truth is bullied into a corner and demonised. The world is now becoming deaf to the saving cry of the truth. Yet with gentleness and warmth, we must love and witness amidst all this. In this sense, whilst the world rejoices, we mourn.

"Truly, truly, I say to you, you will weep and lament, the world will rejoice; you will be sorrowful, but your sorrow will turn into joy" (John 16:20). As Jesus drew close to the end of His earthly ministry, one of the things He made sure to make clear to the disciples was the reality of the inevitability of the Christian cross. *"Narrow is the path,"* He says. So, in the above scriptural text, Jesus reminds His disciples of the impending sorrow which will then turn to joy. I think that the most important thing to note here is that sorrow will only turn to joy if the Christian has lived the reality of the sorrow with all it brings. The Christian joy, therefore, can be said to be accessed through the cross. It flows from and goes beyond the cross to eternal blessedness. The path of the cross is privileged and a gift because God's choice of us and our free assent to His choice now takes us through a sorrow whose definite end is joy. *"On account of me, they will do all these things to you"* (John 15:21). In other words, because of Jesus, we will live this Christian reality with all its tensions and contradictions. And yet, through it, God has wrought His saving power (1 Corinthians 1:18).

Simeon prophesied and foretold Jesus' path of contradiction and said, *"Behold this child is set for the fall and the rising of many in Israel and for a sign that is spoken against (and a sword will pierce through your own soul also) that thoughts out of many hearts may be revealed"* (Luke 2:34-35).

Paradoxically, the Prince of Peace that comes to save now becomes a contradiction, a cause for the piercing of the heart of Mother Mary. In Him, we find everything: the rising and the fall of many, vicious criticisms, and *"He will be spoken against."* But interestingly, it is precisely within these contradictory realities that the secret thoughts of many will be revealed for their salvation. Thus, Christianity, which is an encounter with the person of Jesus, is shrouded in these contradictions, *"for a servant is not greater than the master"* (John 15:20).

It then follows that our witnessing and remaining true to His choice of us is firstly about being faithful within it and the contradictions it brings. Jesus' ministry would have been a failure if He aimed to avoid these contradictions. In fact, for Jesus, these contradictions were invitations and an existential character of His mission of dispelling darkness (John 1:5), a process which often causes offence.

Dealing with the offence

Does this then mean that the Christian is unconcerned about the offence our faith causes others? Not in the least. The Christian is called to maintain the bond of peace and to be at peace with all people. Therefore, this offence that is naturally provoked by authentic Christian living, becomes part of the crosses we must carry and the tensions within which we must live. Our proclamation of the Gospel is not without offence and tension. Although these offences are not necessary, they are often direct consequences of the Gospel's truthfulness to its salvific mission.

Soren Kierkegaard, in his work on Christian training, summarises the truth of these present contradictions and tensions. He says, "Take away the possibility of offence, as they have done in Christendom, and the whole of Christianity is direct communication; and then Christianity is done away with, for it has become an easy thing, a superficial something which neither wounds nor heals profoundly enough; it is the false invention of human sympathy which forgets the infinite qualitative difference between God and man."[20]

---

[20] Søren Kierkegaard, *"Training in Christianity; And the Edifying Discourse which Accompanied it" Trans. By Walter Lowrie.* Princeton University Press, 2015. *Project MUSE* muse.jhu.edu/book/42828.

For Kierkegaard, as much as the Christian is called to be polite and peaceful, the very nature of the encounter of the world with his faith makes this impossible to eliminate offence in the pursuit of the truth. The Christian life is a witness and a light that confronts the darkness of sin and ignorance which hold the world in captivity. For Kierkegaard, to the world, this offence is an inherent nature of the Christian witness. But for the believer, it is a sign that the world needs saving. He seems to invite us to the knowledge that makes us quit trying to make the faith conform to our human way of thinking, where everything has to be logical. When we ignore this knowledge/truth, this false human sympathy takes over, and, in his words, we "forget the infinite qualitative difference between God and man." It seems to me that when Jesus talked about carrying our cross and following Him, He meant all of these. He doesn't want us to try to eliminate the cross to create a human-invented religion based simply on sympathy but with no power to save.

William McDavid wondered where in particular this offence is and what exactly it is. He says, "If you are an 'absolute paradox,' to use Kierkegaard's word, or a 'stumbling-block,' to use St Paul's, then to be understood is often to be misunderstood."[21] The reality of these offences and contradictions was there in Jesus' teachings, of course not because Jesus delighted in offensiveness. Thus, William McDavid thought that "A sermon which does not arouse this offence in the preacher, a book which does not arouse it in its author, a politics which does not arouse it in the Christian political class, threatens to become a mere human invention, one which does not wound or heal in the profound way envisioned by Kierkegaard. That's maybe one reason why Christianity always has a place for the ironic, the playful, the subversive, all modes of indirect communication."

I must immediately say here that Christianity is founded on the principle of charity and all the fruits of the Holy Spirit. This means that a Christian message cannot remain a Christian message if it is aimed at offending others or if every attempt within reason is not made to make any possible or envisaged offence bearable. The Holy Spirit is gentleness but also the Spirit of truth. This means that the truth is communicated in gentleness. Yet it does not mean that some truths

---

[21] William McDavid, "Kierkegaard on (Lost) Offense of Christianity" 2016, Kierkegaard on the (Lost) Offense of Christianity - Mockingbird (mbird.com)

of the Christian faith will not be offensive, at least at the initial stage of conveying them.

The offence is often from the wounds

Noteworthy is the fact that the offence is often not from the truth itself but from our wounds. Thus, when touched by the truth, there is a stirring of what is perceived as pain. The attempt to communicate the faith in a way that eliminates all offence is something even Jesus couldn't do, so He could remain true to Himself and His purpose. While the pains, confusion and frustrations the people felt often made Jesus' heart very heavy and laden with pity, He nonetheless knew that this offence was not the thing, but an indicator of His people's need for healing. Jesus knew that it was part of the process of healing and being saved. Thus, Kierkegaard thought that to, "take away this possibility of offence, simply makes the Christian faith something superficial that neither wounds nor heals profoundly enough." In the wounds lies the invitation for healing. Offence in this case could be evidence of existent wounds which the sufferer is often unaware of. The encounter with Christian witnessing brings this up and calls it to healing. Eliminate the offence, then the wounds and our needs for healing are concealed. Consequently, the Christian faith is stripped of its depth and indeed its power to heal.

To hold on firmly to the faith amid all these pressures, we must remember that God's choice of us has separated us from the world so that we may be able to witness to the world by living in that tense encounter which often leaves us confused, uncertain, maybe with a feeling of guilt for not being considerate and sensitive enough, and often misunderstood. These feelings can be very powerful and crippling. You would have noticed how these experiences have weakened a lot of pastors of souls who certainly loved the flock entrusted to them and would do everything to alleviate their pains. Unfortunately, to deal with it, some of us pastors have made the easy choice of not talking about certain areas of the faith. Certain words are eliminated, and some teachings of Christ are completely avoided. But this attempt to eliminate every offence is illusory and impossible. The very act of eliminating or avoiding these truths is already an offence to many. If the pastor's decision to avoid offence is strictly for the sake of the flock, then effort should also be made to alleviate the offence felt by those others who feel that the elimination or avoidance of certain teachings is offensive. After all, they are also part of his flock. Now, where does that leave us if not in tension?

The path I would like to propose here is not a middle ground but rather to faithfully discern how best to present the authenticity of the gospel with all its possibility of offence. This is precisely why the preaching of the gospel is a hard call. Convenience is not the principle that guides the Christian gospel, neither is an offence. On the contrary, love is the guiding principle. And if it is true love, it is bound to hurt or offend sometimes. Eliminate every possibility of offence, then true love becomes an illusion, impossible to live by imperfect human beings.

To truly live the gospel is to live in the purifying fire of the cross, the faith and the truth. This fire purifies just as it tests us. One may ask, "Does it not get easier?" Of course, it does. But only by a conscious striving to embrace the truth even with all its offences and the contradictions, and then within it, try to know, understand and trust. It is a cross, a yoke, but of righteousness, which is lighter than the yoke of sin. *"For my yoke is easier and my burden is light."* [22] The deeper we get into the process, the less turbulence these contradictions cause our lives. They do not go away, but we can rise higher into the clouds of faith, while being grounded on its firm foundation, where growth is high as well as the risks. This is the process to spiritual stability.

---

[22] Matt. 11:30

Chapter Five

THE SCANDAL OF PERFECT LOVE

God's love: the Christian firm foundation

For God so loved the world that he gave his only Son, that whoever believes in him should not die but have eternal life (John 3:16).

The victorious Christian life can only be attained by being grounded in the knowledge and experience of God's love. Amid these confusions and misunderstandings of what we are about, love becomes the force that impels us, driving us through what is often a dark, narrow path. God's love fills us and makes us firmly grounded against the tide of these scandals through which the

Christian must walk. For this reason, St. Paul writes to the Christian community in Ephesus and prays that they may *"comprehend the breadth and length and height and depth of God's love, that being rooted and grounded in love, they may be filled with the fullness of God"* (Ephesians 3:14-19). This love must be at the core of our hearts and being if we are to live faithfully and fruitfully.

A priest once told a story of how, after he had given a homily at Mass, a parishioner accosted him and said, "Father, thank you for saying something else that isn't about love this and love that." You would wonder if the man didn't want to hear about God's love, or maybe he had problems with the reality of God's love, or perhaps with the way God's love had been preached, maybe in a very abstract and flowery way.

To appreciate what I am about to say here, it is important we know the context of this conversation. The priest was talking about how preachers throw the idea of God's love around in such a reckless way that it almost renders the believer very passive in what should be an active relationship of love. Often, the idea of God's love is instrumentalised to indulge and exonerate oneself or people from the responsibility and the openness that love, in its very nature, necessarily demands. A person once said that he had realised that when preachers do not know what to preach, perhaps due to unpreparedness, they simply tell the people that God loves them, only phrasing it differently.

Indeed, nothing is wrong with reminding us every day that we are loved by God. We need to remind ourselves of that fundamental and foundational truth. So, there can never be too much talking of God's love. However, the truth of God's love must be presented in a way that does not betray its very nature and make it meaningless and boring to hear. Neither should it be wrongly and recklessly thrown about in a way that renders the Christian idle and passive. Certainly, there is no passivity in a loving relationship.

I remember speaking with a young pastor years ago, and he said something that was rather shocking but at the same time an eye-opener as to how an aspect of the truth could be so wrongly emphasised to the expense of the other aspects of the same truth perhaps with a pius intent of eliminating these existent tensions or contradictions in our faith. He said something along these lines, "Chinedu, I am a child of God, a new creation.[23] Therefore, I cannot sin."[24] At first, I struggled to understand what he meant. Obviously, I knew where he was quoting from the Scripture. But I wanted to understand if he meant that he didn't sin and shouldn't choose to remain in sin or if he truly meant it literally, that he did not sin at all. But he told me bluntly, "I cannot sin even if I fornicated. It is not me, but my sinful nature."[25]

One can perceive a deadly dualism here. I was hit by the realisation that such an understanding of God's forgiveness and love is existent in the Church of God on earth. Yes, it is good to powerfully and radically announce the merits of the life, death and resurrection of Jesus Christ. It is indeed what we are called to do with conviction and authority. But care must be taken to announce these immeasurable merits of the cross with true knowledge and humility. We cannot, however, announce the merits of the cross in such a way that renders it meaningless, powerless and boring to assent to.

In the face of the nonchalant misinterpretation of the word "love" in our world today, it is very important we talk about God's love today. According to Pope Emeritus Benedict XVI, "God's

---
[23] 2 Corinthians 5:17
[24] 1 John 3:9
[25] Romans 7:17

love for us is fundamental for our lives, and it raises important questions about who God is and who we are." [26] Benedict XVI seems to suggest that the reality of God's love is fundamental to understanding who God is and who we are. To know God's love then is to know God and who we are, considering love as a mode of knowledge.

While I wish to announce here God's love as the Christian's firm foundation and driving force, I do not in the least wish to render it meaningless, boring and powerless by sacrificing its demands. Neither do I intend to render the Christian passive in this act of loving. However, we must say that God's love, in its very nature, remains the same whether we are passive or not. It is not a consequence of any response on our part, but to appropriate its power, the Christian cannot remain passive.

First, we are creatures of love. We were created in love by Love because God is love.[27] Having created us in love, God destined us to a life of love because God, who is love, is our destiny and end. Therefore, when humanity fell from the life of grace due to sin (Genesis 3) and as a consequence,

---
[26] Benedict XVI, Deus Caritas Est, (Rome: Libreria Editrice Vaticana, 2005, p.2
[27] 1 John 4:8

rejected the Love that had always loved them, God did not relent in His love. Why? God has always loved us with an everlasting love (Jeremiah 31:3).

The consequence of the sin of humanity was such that we couldn't help ourselves. Our condition was indeed dire. The reality of this situation has been given various descriptions by different authors and theologians. Many called it a state of hopelessness and darkness. Why do I need to press so hard on this state of humanity without salvation in Christ, while our topic of focus is God's love? This is the point I try to make. The love of God remains the same and is always constant, with or without the coming of Jesus Christ. The coming of Christ, however, became a powerful manifestation and restoration of the knowledge and the splendour of that love, which providentially was revealed in our darkest moment to dispel our darkness.[28]

St. Athanasius work on Incarnation explains this more clearly:

"For God had made man thus (that is, as an embodied spirit), and had willed that he should remain in incorruption. But men, having turned from the

---

[28] John 1:5. In the prologue of John the Eternal Word that comes into the world, steeped in darkness, shines forth so brightly that it overpowers the darkness.

contemplation of God to evil of their own devising, had come inevitably under the law of death. Instead of remaining in the state in which God had created them, they were in process of becoming corrupted entirely, and death had them completely under its dominion. For the transgression of the commandment was making them turn back again according to their nature; and as they had at the beginning come into being out of non-existence, so were they now on the way to returning, through corruption, to non-existence again. The presence and love of the Word had called them into being; inevitably, therefore, when they lost the knowledge of God, they lost existence with it; for it is God alone Who exists, evil is non-being, the negation and antithesis of good. By nature, of course, man is mortal, since he was made from nothing; but he bears also the Likeness of Him Who is, and if he preserves that Likeness through constant contemplation, then his nature is deprived of its power and he remains incorrupt. So is it affirmed in Wisdom: "The keeping of His laws is the assurance of incorruption." And being incorrupt, he would be henceforth as God, as Holy Scripture says, "I have said, Ye are gods and sons of the Highest all of you: but ye die as men and fall as one of the princes." This, then, was the plight of men. God had not only made them out of nothing, but had also graciously bestowed on them His own life by the grace of the Word. Then, turning from eternal things to things corruptible, by counsel of the devil, they had become the cause of their own corruption in death; for, as I said before, though they were by nature subject to corruption, the grace of their union with the Word made them capable of escaping from the natural law, provided that they retained the beauty of innocence with which they were created. That is to say, the presence of the Word with them shielded them even from natural corruption, as also Wisdom says: "God created man for incorruption and as an image of His own eternity; but by envy of the devil death entered into the world." When this happened, men began to die, and corruption ran riot among them and held sway over them to an even more than natural degree, because it was the penalty of which God had forewarned them for transgressing the commandment. Indeed, they had in their sinning surpassed all limits; for having invented wickedness in the beginning and so involved themselves in death and corruption, they had gone on gradually from bad to worse, not stopping at any one kind of evil, but continually, as with insatiable appetite, devising new kinds of sins. Adulteries and thefts were everywhere, murder and raping filled the earth, law was disregarded in corruption and injustice, all kinds of iniquities were perpetrated by all, both singly and in common. Cities were warring with cities, nations were rising against nations, and the whole earth was rent with factions and battles, while each strove to outdo the other in wickedness. Even crimes contrary to nature were not unknown, but as the martyr-apostle of Christ says: "Their women changed the natural use into that which is against nature; and the men also, leaving the natural use of the woman, flamed out in lust towards each other, perpetrating shameless acts with their own sex, and receiving in their own persons the due recompense of their perverseness"."[29]

St. Athanasius then talked about what he called the dilemma of God. In his words, "It was unthinkable that God should go back upon his words and that man, having transgressed, should not die; but it was equally monstrous that beings which once had shared the nature of the Word should perish and turn back again into non-existence through corruption."[30] This is where it gets even more interesting. St. Athanasius rightly thought and said that, "It was unworthy of the goodness of God that creatures made by God should be brought to nothing through the deceit

---

[29] St Athanasius, *On Incarnation*, (Rome: Libreria Editrice Vaticana, 2005, p.1-57
[30] St Athanasius, *On Incarnation,* Translated and edited by a Religious of SPCK, 2008, p.1-57

wrought by the devil; and it was supremely unfitting that the work of God in mankind should disappear."[31]

To cut a long story short, to reconcile this dilemma, the incorporeal and incorruptible and immaterial Word of God entered our world (See John 1). The Lord condescended and took on flesh, a body that was prepared for Him, so that in dying for us, God would have saved us and yet remained faithful to His words, which means that death would have had its full course. This is what 1 John 4:9 meant when it says that God's love was made manifest when He sent His son, *"that through Christ Jesus we may live"* (John 3:17).

Pope Benedict XVI described this timely intervention of God's love in his work, "Deus Caritas Est." He says,

"This *agape* dimension of God's love for man goes far beyond the aspect of gratuity. Israel has committed 'adultery' and has broken the covenant; God should judge and repudiate her. It is precisely at this point that God is revealed to be God and not man: 'How can I give you up, O Ephraim! How can I hand you over, O Israel! ...My

---

[31] St Athanasius, *On* Incarnation, Translated and edited by a Religious of SPCK, 2008, P.6

heart recoils within me. My compassion grows warm and tender. I will not execute my fierce anger. I will not again destroy Ephraim; for I am God and not man, the Holy One in your midst' (*Hos* 11:8-9). God's passionate love for his people—for humanity—is at the same time a forgiving love. It is so great that it turns God against himself, his love against his justice. Here Christians can see a dim prefiguration of the mystery of the Cross: so great is God's love for man that by becoming man he follows him even into death, and so reconciles justice and love."[32]

What we find as we reflect on God's love is how the sin of humanity constantly pushes the boundaries to exhaust God's love, but only to be overcome by God's love at the climactic point and height when the only things left would have been judgement and repudiation due to her sins. Instead of the sins of humanity wearing God's love out, the reverse is always the case.

In all I have been saying so far, one can see that the divine initiative to save humanity was not orchestrated by any merits on the part of humanity, nor was it for anything we had done. It

---

[32] Benedict XVI, *Deus Caritas Est*, (Rome: Libreria Editrice Vaticana, 2005 p.10

was simply for God's love, which is completely independent of our love for him. Hence the Bible says that God has loved us first.[33] What we are talking about here is a love that precedes our creation and the foundation of the world, and thus shows us how faithful and unshakable that love has been and will always be.[34] There is nothing here to suggest that we were the ones begging God to love and save us. Rather, we see a God thirsty for our salvation and who runs to us to save us. For while we were still weak, sinners and enemies of God, at the right time, Christ died for us.[35]

This truth of personal knowledge of God's love is fundamental and foundational to Christian living. I intentionally qualified this love and knowledge as *personal* just to emphasise the needed level of appropriation of that truth. God loves every one of us personally and is willing to go to any length for the love He has for us. He has shown this through the gifting of His son, Jesus (John. 3:16). On account of this, St. John says, *"So, we know and believe the love God has for us."*

---

[33] 1 John 4:19
[34] Ephesians 1:3-14
[35] Romans 5:6,10. St Paul presents in a very power way the gratuitousness of the Salvation in Christ, thus bringing out more clearly the unconditional character of God's love towards.

The Christian life, I dare to say, can only be lived faithfully with the knowledge of this truth, that is, the experience and the knowledge of God's love. There may be times when circumstances push us so hard to question this truth, but the experience we have had of this love in the past, impressed upon our heart through the power of the Holy Spirit, sustains us. The knowledge of God's love sustains in us a victorious Christian life. We are invited to walk in that love every day. I am not talking now about our love for God, but His love for us. We are to walk in that knowledge of being loved, perfectly and unconditionally accepted every day and every moment. This is the love that scares away fears (1 John 4:18). This love is our hope, strength and our drive. It is our strength because even when all fails, we know that God's love will never fail. It is completely independent of this changing world and eternally transcends the vicissitude of this created order. Even in the most difficult situation, we can count on the Eternal Father's love, as Jesus did even upon the cross and say, "Into your hands, I commend my spirit." We hope to live today in love and forever in its promised glorious future, which is built on God's constant love (Psalm 100:5). And we are sure of this hope since it is born of God's spirit of love.[36]

God's love urges us on

God's love is our essence. The Scripture says that the love of God urges us on (2 Corinthians 5:14-15). This Scripture has many implications, but I will highlight just two of them. The first is that it is the love of God that must move us, that is, if we are to move in the right direction till the end. It is not our love that moves us because ours always falls short and is rarely uncontaminated. The second is that we are then to walk in this love daily. It should be the fire in our hearts and bones (Jeremiah 20:19).

A victorious Christian life would be impossible in the face of the tensions and contradictions discussed in the previous chapter if one does not stand firm on the knowledge of God's love. We are to let God's love lead us rather than the forces of our circumstances and situations. Let His love drive our prayer life so that our prayers will not wear us out and avail very little.

In Christ, we are divinely summoned to be aflame by God's love for us if we are to overcome the guilt

---

[36] Romans 5:5

of our past. The knowledge of this truth tells us that God's love for us is bigger than our shame and iniquity (Colossians 12-13). God's love tells us that, *"God has made us alive together with him, having forgiven us all our trespasses, having cancelled the bond which stood against us with its legal demands. This he set aside, nailing it to the cross. He disarmed the principalities and powers and made public examples of them, triumphing over them in him"* (Colossians 2:13-15).

Knowing full well that in Christ we are a new creation (2 Corinthians 5:17) and that there is no condemnation unto us who are in Christ Jesus (Romans 8:1), we confidently face not just our past but more importantly our future. Considering what helpless and hopeless situations we have been saved from, we cannot but ask ourselves, *"What can separate us now from his love? If God is for us, who can be against us? He who did not spare his only Son but gave him up for us all, will he not give us all things with him? Who shall separate us from the love of Christ? Shall tribulations, or distress or persecutions or famine or nakedness or peril or sword? No, in all these things we are more than conquerors through him who loved us."* We must understand that what has been done for us and in us through Christ cannot be undone. St. Paul described this reality as being transferred from the dominion of darkness to the kingdom of God's beloved son in whom we have redemption, the forgiveness of sins.

Drawing from the above, we can see that much has indeed been given to us. And to whom much is given, much is expected. Even more so, to whom much is freely and unconditionally given, much more is expected. God's love immediately, and as a consequence of our appropriation of it, impels us to act in love and extend this life of love to others. The former must translate to the latter if we are to truly appropriate God's love. Every Christian comes alive in love, just like faith is only alive through love. All other Christian virtues would be dead if they were not driven by love, not necessarily our love for God but God's love for us.

God is the source of our love

When I was a chaplain to the homelessness charity, I had the opportunity to deal with many traumatised people. Most would have been homeless, traumatised, sick and with mental health problems as well. I would usually organise prayer sessions on Tuesdays for anyone who might be inclined to attend. As you can imagine, having a prayer meeting with people confronting such difficult situations can be quite adventurous and insightful because you are not sure what to expect.

I remember in one of our prayer sessions, we discussed the theme of love using 1 Corinthians 13:1-8,13. The sessions were usually kept very simple and safe for everyone to freely participate without feeling pressured. Within the session, we had a time when everyone was invited to share their thoughts, insights, questions or any concerns about the readings. That was the big moment because you get what you get. Being able to deal with that was the most challenging part of the sessions. So, on this occasion, one of the participants, unknown to me, struggled with the word "love." After we had read the scripture about love being patient, kind, and all that, he said, "I have experienced love in my life. I know what love is and how powerful it can be. All those emotions and energy and being drawn to the other in love. But when we talk about loving God, I don't feel that way. I have tried but couldn't. Besides, all that love does, in the end, is to hurt and bring you down because it fades away at some point. It doesn't stay." When he was done, the others in attendance and I were quiet for a while.

At first, I could see the sincerity and profundity in his sharing. Of course, it was his experience. Now I remember that before he started, I had said something like, "Love is a beautiful thing." In hindsight now, I think that was what triggered him. I clearly remember how he looked at me and laughed before he started talking. Reflecting quickly on what he said, I was very much aware that it was not everybody's experience of love or God's love. However, what he shared was his experience and was true for him. Secondly, I acknowledged his experience as true but also saw the need to lead him to consider why that was the case. What I noticed as he spoke was some kind of suspicion whenever the word love was mentioned. In fact, at some point, he said that he suspected that love was a negative or demonic force that in the end only hurts or destroys. It took us time to dissect and to get to a point where I could direct him to God's love towards us rather than his love for God.

At the closing prayer, I emphasised God's love towards us. Something happened as I said that prayer, and when I finished, I saw his eyes were red. He was holding back tears. I could sense a change of emotion there. What it was, I wasn't sure, until he called me and said, "Father, you know what, while you were praying, I felt God's love for the first time."

We see now how central and fundamental the contemplation of God's love is in our journey of faith. It is the knowledge, contemplation and experience of God's love that bear the fruit of our love for God. Our love for God stands directly upon His love for us. Otherwise, it cannot stand. Our love is always weak and has the tendency to fluctuate, whilst God's is constant. That is what this participant meant when he said that love fades very quickly and doesn't last. And that can be true about our love for each other, especially when stretched beyond the end of our strength.

However, the love with which the Christian loves God and the neighbour is God's love poured into our hearts (Romans 5:5). This is what makes God's love, not our love, the premise and foundation of our relationship with God. At this point, you probably understand why I wondered what it was with the man who was concerned about the incessant preaching of God's love in the Church. Listen, I would argue that the Christian will profit very little, if anything at all, in our Christian journey without the knowledge of God's love. The Christian journey is a lifelong voyage of constant discovery and rediscovery of God's love. That's why a Christian's growth in faith is rightly measured by one's love, a fruit borne from the knowledge of God's love. Hence, the Bible says, love each other as I have loved you. God's love is the reference point, the source, the sustenance and indeed the *telos* of our lives.

The invitation

The first thing we are called to do is to believe and accept this love and then act on it. That was what Jesus tried to explain to Martha in the Gospel of John. There, Jesus came to Bethany where his friend Lazarus had died, and four days had already passed. As Jesus spoke with Martha, He said to her, *"Did I not ask you that if you believe, you will see the salvation of the Lord?"* In other words, Jesus was inviting Martha to accept the love that has loved us freely but is irresistibly intense. She was being invited to witness the power of God's love to save, to believe and to act, based on who God is and what He says. Jesus knew that naturally, Martha was hindered by the common knowledge that once one is dead, he or she is dead. And to make the matter worse, four days had already passed. But He called her to believe God's report and to abandon herself in God's hands. Jesus then said to her, *"I am the resurrection and the life."*

Surprisingly, as Jesus prayed, He began to weep. Jesus' weeping remains an image of His high priestly intercession for us, flowing from a heart burning in love for us. Hence, the Letter to the Hebrews 5:7 says that **during Jesus' life on earth, He offered up prayers and petitions with fervent cries and tears. Jesus still offers for us intercessions flowing from a deep place of love. And we know that His intercession can save.**

Praying for a fresh experience of God's love

If there is anything we ought to be praying for at this time, it is for a fresh and profound experience of God's love because this is the driving force for the Christian mission and life. Without a deep knowledge and experience of this love, our faith becomes mere religiosity, void of its power, meaning and purpose. Therefore, we mistakenly labour to merit God's love instead of submitting to the truth that we can't merit such love by any deeds of ours. The love that has loved us in this way is beyond what humanity can merit. Rather, we deepen our knowledge of this love every day and learn to act as he urges us.

Being Filled by God

To be filled by God or to remain full of God is to be filled by His love or rather the awareness or knowledge of His love (see John 17:26, Ephesian 3:19), and when we are filled with the truth and experience of this love, we shall not be overcome by anything, even if the struggles endure. Yes, we may be wounded and struck down many times, but because of His love, we will be raised up. We cannot be destroyed because our fate has already been sealed in Him, as long as we anchor on His love, in knowing and in doing. This is indeed the way the Lord has loved the world so much that He gave Himself in His only begotten son that whosoever believes in Him should not perish but have eternal life. (John 3:16).

God's love is indeed our hope, shield, and our strength. When we are down and unable to take the next step, God's love encourages us and becomes our life anchor. Our lives, like a ship, may sometimes be tossed about by the torrents of life. God's love is the only anchor and the mast. Our faith in those moments must be faith working through love (Galatians 5:6).

When we are weighed down by our pasts or held in grave situations of sin, God's love is our hope as we make our way from the valley and darkness of sin to the mount and light of truth. Only by our trust in His truth and love can we not run out of patience with ourselves, others and indeed God. Our religious activities then, be it prayers, service to the poor, going to and helping out in the Church, etc. ought to be fuelled by the knowledge of God's love, since that is what gives the Christian act its definite character and power.

I just thought I should end this section by focusing on St. Paul's prayer for the Christian community in Ephesians 3:14-19.

"For this reason, I bow my knees before the Father, from whom every family in heaven and on earth is named, that according to the riches of his glory, he may grant you to be strengthened with might through his Spirit in the inner man, and that Christ may dwell in your hearts

through faith, that you being rooted and grounded in love may have power to comprehend with all the saints what is the breadth and length and height and depth and to know the love of Christ which surpasses knowledge that you may be filled with all the fullness of God."

While our faith may sometimes throw us into what could be described as a spiritual crucible, we must affirm very strongly that God's love is stronger than anything that may come our way. A heart that has already found in God a true lover and treasure will faithfully live the paradoxes and scandals of faith with an assurance of our non-deceptive hope born of the Holy Spirit through love. This hope, nonetheless, is only appropriated through suffering and patience—waiting for its timely actualisation (Romans 5:1-5). But how could we wait had we not been impelled by love? And how could love be lived if it is void of the Christian hope that we must await because of its certainty? It is in the character of the Christian hope to summon us to the Christian waiting. Hence, in the next chapter, we shall look at Christian waiting as a necessary path, if we are to fruitfully and faithfully live the Christian life.

Chapter Six

THE CHRISTIAN WAITING

We mostly think of waiting in our everyday lives and experiences as an idle, boring and sometimes frustrating moment. Waiting almost appears to us as a fruitless time because, as humans, we are not always aware of the inner workings of grace and the supernatural in the ordinary. Often, we have received more in the process of waiting than at any other time. In most cases, it is during waiting that the often unseen foundations of most things, projects, vocations and dreams are laid and the man or woman prepared to face life.

Christian waiting can be very hard. But with the right kind of attitude, the process of waiting can be a very fruitful time, in as much as it remains very sacrificial, especially if one does not know when what is being awaited is to be accomplished or fulfilled. However, Christian waiting is anchored on faith and hope. Thus, the Letter to the Hebrews describes faith as the evidence of things hoped for and the conviction of things not seen. For the Christian then, waiting upon God's promises isn't idling about. It is indeed a process, an action, an act of faith to be precise. And within that process of faithful waiting, we are changed and transformed.

Even though our Christian waiting is anchored on things we have not seen, it is not purposeless. It is certain because it is anchored on the Christian hope which is born of God's love poured into our hearts through the Holy Spirit. Therefore, we patiently and confidently await the fulfilment of our hopes, whilst praying with the Psalmist in Psalm 119, *"Uphold me by your promises and do not disappoint me in my hopes."*

Our waiting is purposeful, and not idle. It is an act of faith which stands on the faithfulness of the One who makes the promises to come. With the eyes of faith then, we embrace and receive that which our faith and hope look forward to, as our fathers and mothers in faith did, as recorded by the Letter to the Hebrews, chapter 11. Since Christian waiting isn't idle and fruitless, we keep busy working, as our Father is working to accomplish what He has promised. We go on taking steps and living, based on the assurance of what we wait for.

Christian waiting is an active process because living in hope places a demand on us. No wonder the Bible says in 1 John 3:3 that those who entertain this hope should therefore purify themselves. Here, we see hope and action working together. Christian waiting engages us to prepare us for what we wait for. Hence, the Gospel of Luke, 12 says, *"See that you are dressed for action and have your lamps lit. Be like men waiting for their master to return."* Jesus ends the discourse by adding, *"You too must stand ready because the Son of Man is coming at an hour you do not expect"* (Luke 12).

Therefore, Christian waiting requires active engagement, watchfulness and a prayerful waiting, symbolised by having our lamps lit as Jesus tells us in Luke 12. Knowing that our hope cannot disappoint, as good stewards, we know that God will make good His promises in His time of visitation. So, we remain awake and on our guard, waiting for the Lord's advent.

To reiterate, we are changed in this process. Hence, the Bible says that there is a renewal of strength for those who wait upon the Lord. Like a fire, Christian waiting purifies us from the debris and the darkness that clouds our vision. It burns the heaviness within and raises our heads to gaze on that which is set above. But this requires time. In this process of waiting, we come to know ourselves better and are trained on patient endurance, with which the Bible says we redeem our souls (Luke 21:19). It is sacrificial, but it bears great enduring fruits of righteousness.

Christian waiting could be likened to the process of dying, like a seed under the soil which then germinates and navigates through the soil to the surface. I don't imagine this process to be easy, at least not more than it would have been for the seed sown in the soil. But the seed doesn't really have any choice if it must survive and live. The only alternative is to remain there and eventually wither. We too, when we find ourselves in the depth of waiting, have only one choice if we are to be alive spiritually, and that is to wait, for as long as it takes. Our forebears in faith waited. Without having received what was promised to them, they trusted and from afar, welcomed it. They accepted that they were pilgrims looking for a permanent homeland, a city whose foundation is God.

You can see that Christian waiting is by no means idle and boring; it can be sacrificially adventurous. We keep being drawn and impelled by God's love in our hearts, not to let go, but to keep going. Even though the object of our waiting may delay, based on the human perception of timing, we wait for it because of God's faithfulness. Like our fathers and mothers in faith (see Hebrews 11), even if our eyes become weak because of age, we are to hold onto our hope by faith, recognising that we are simply pilgrims passing through this temporary life. We look forward to an eternal city, our heavenly home. This waiting is, as it were, enfleshed by the understanding of the truth that we are pilgrims on earth. There are promises made to us that we may not see completion in the flesh. We may only see its beginning but not its flourishing or completion. But through the eyes of faith, we welcome it, not feeling disappointed by God. When we truly see ourselves as pilgrims on earth and act as such, there is a sense in which we become aware that we are not just a person but part of a people. Hence, many promises of God that come to us, in their very nature, look beyond us and sometimes beyond our immediate families.

This illustration might help us understand better. The Lord had promised Abraham an heir and to make his descendants as many as the stars of heaven. Even before then, Abraham had trusted in God's words and left behind his land and everything he had known and had. With the passage of time, and as Abraham advanced in age with his wife, he began to feel that time was running out on him. As a human, he would have wondered, "When will God fulfil this promise? Is it when I am incapable of having a child or even dead?" When we think that God's promises are simply for us alone and end with us, we fail to see their implications on generations to come and when we fail to see beyond ourselves in God's promises, it is quite easy to entertain the lie that God might not keep His promises. It seems to me that this was what happened to Abraham and made him run out of patience and go ahead of God, perhaps to help hasten up the promise. He ended up going to the maid, Haggai, who gave him a son, Ishmael.

But then, God reminds and corrects him that what he has done was not in any way a fulfilment of what had been promised, which shall be fulfilled in its time. Finally, the Lord fulfilled His promise and gave him a son of promise, Isaac. The Lord would later ask him to sacrifice this son. He obeyed, but it was simply a test and a foreshadowing of what was to be fulfilled in Christ, the only begotten Son of God, who would be sacrificed as the true lamb and a son of promise upon whom all the promises of God stand to say yes. For Abraham to have accepted to sacrifice Isaac, the son of promise, suggests that he must have understood and accepted that the plan of God was simply way beyond him and his concern of having a child to carry on his lineage. When we read the Scripture, we see that the fulfilment of God's promise and plans for Abraham were nowhere near to completion. He had seen the beginning, signalled by the birth of Isaac, but its fulfilment, when the world would bless themselves by him (Abraham), and his descendants being as many as the stars, these promised moments looked beyond him. Please, think about all this as we wait for God's promises.

Waiting in openness

If you think for a moment about the hopes held by

ancient Israel, which were founded on God's promises to Abraham for a land, nation, kingdom and of blessedness, and if you consider in what ways these promises were fulfilled and are still being fulfilled now in Christ, sometimes in the most unexpected ways, you cannot but see how important openness during the time of waiting can be. There you have promises which now lead to hope - hope for their fulfilment. Within this perceived gap between promises and fulfilment, the waiting of God's people takes on a definite character of Abraham's prophecy in Genesis 22:8: *"God himself will provide the lamb for the burnt offering, my son."*

Here you have a man whose hope for the continuity of his lineage lay in his only son, whom he had been asked to sacrifice. Most certainly, he must have been confused and worried about what God was up to. The likely question would have been, "If I sacrifice Isaac, how then will God's promises be fulfilled?" So, for Abraham, there was a complete uncertainty, a "cloud of unknowing." But his only way out of this situation, which was actually a test, was to remain open. As he gave that prophecy about God Himself providing a lamb, he keyed into what would later become the dream and hope of ancient Israel, and indeed of all humanity, an expectation of the true Lamb. *"For on his mountain, the Lord will provide."* And finally, on the mount of Calvary, the Lord provided the true and unblemished Lamb, Jesus.

For Abraham and the generations after him and before Christ, how the Lord would do this remained unknown. Hence, there was great need for openness, lest they miss their time of visitation. Unfortunately, as we know it, the opposite happened. God's people were not very open. Thus, when the true Lamb was finally provided, the true Lamb of sacrifice, the Lamb that takes away their sins and those of the whole world, they didn't recognise Him. John 1 says that He came to His own, and His own people did not accept Him.

As the Bible says, all these things were written for us to learn, to be taught, instructed, guided by them so that we who believe may be fully equipped unto good works (2 Timothy 3:17). It takes openness for us to recognise the fulfilment of the object of our hopes, and in this case, the promises of God. God keeps His promises, but their fulfilment is often in the most unexpected ways. The coming of Jesus was meant to be the fulfilment of the ancient hopes of God's people. It is in Him that God is gathering all nations to Himself, establishing a new covenant; in Him, God is establishing an everlasting kingdom. In Him, who is the root and stock of Jesse, God is bringing about the blessedness of all people, for through Him an offer of blessedness will be made to the whole world.

God's people failed to receive Him since they were unable to recognise Him. However, they couldn't recognise Him because they were somewhat closed to the ways of God which are often not our ways, and whose thoughts are not our thoughts (Isaiah 55:8-9). Without openness to God's logic, the fulfilment of God's promises falls short of our misguided expectations. And when that happens, we could be staring at the time of visitation without knowing.

So, the Christian waits with openness, knowing fully that the fulfilment of God's promises goes beyond the person and extends to generations after. The Christian knows that what is at stake isn't just about them and understands that God retains the freedom of when and in what way to accomplish what he has promised. The fact that we do not know when and how shouldn't weigh us down. Rather, it should lead us to preparedness, knowing that we are changed in the waiting process. Hence, Christian waiting isn't a moment of idling for God, nor is it so for the Christian. Indeed, the waiting is already part of the fulfilment.

It is in Jesus and through faith in Him that Abraham's children will become as many as the stars. To be able to wait in this way, Abraham needed to entertain and believe the truth that his hope was not only in this world (see 1 Corinthians 15:19), and as such, that his life extended beyond this earthly life, which, though treasured, must be considered a passing stage, *un camino,* on which he was simply a pilgrim.

Consider reflecting on this truth alongside your waiting for God's promise, and you will see what a difference it makes. It isn't going to eliminate the whole difficulty of waiting, but it gives our Christian waiting a new, fresh perspective, which can be reinvigorating.

CONCLUSION

This truth of the contradictions in the Christian faith, I think, should always be witnessed to, preached, correctly understood and accepted, if we are not to continue to experience mass exodus from the faith due to the unintelligibility of our faith. When this truth is not understood, the faithful think that these paradoxes are alien to their faith. As a consequence, they always strive and waste so much energy in trying to get rid of them. And when this becomes impossible, they become frustrated and tired, thinking that it is too much embarrassment. Unfortunately and ignorantly, many leave the Church, thinking their actions are a discovery that will lead to freedom. In the end, and to their disappointment, they discover that, to be true to oneself and to one's deep convictions, Christian or not, contradictions and scandals will never be far from anyone who lives in truth. We are not in control. It cannot all be convenient. We cannot always understand all, and neither can we always be understood. The human person must learn that it is not all about himself or herself. What is at stake is beyond the person.

In the end, we will all recognise that we are never in control. Our sufferings are real and often unavoidable. There are sufferings that must come to us on account of our faith (assent to God's invitation) and God's choice of us. The meeting of these two (our assent and God's invitation/His choice of us) creates a divine-human drama that often leaves us confused about what's happening but, nonetheless, graces each of our experiences, be it good or bad. Indeed, God makes something good out of everything. This seems to be what St. Paul meant when he told the Christian community in Rome that, *"We know that in everything, God works for good with those who love him, who are called according to his purpose"* (Romans 8:28).

Always, the hand of God is upon the life of the Christian who now concretely shares in the sufferings of Christ, so that he or she may share in the glory of Christ (Romans 8:17). However, the Spirit of God helps us to see that, no matter how bad or spectacular our experience of suffering in this life might have been, an experience of His love points to the truth that these sufferings cannot be compared to the glory that will be revealed in us, considering the truth that our experiences aren't all about ourselves. This is important if we are not to miss the bigger picture of our encounters, especially the difficult ones, such as the scandals and contradictions of the cross which we live in and in which alone the world stands the chance of encountering the risen Lord and not some human-invented god without the power to save.

Job's experience points to the truth that God has more at stake in us and in our sufferings than we do. One of the things we learn by the end of the Book of Job is that his sufferings were more about who God is, than about Job and his faithfulness. In the end, God revealed Himself in a way that changed the understanding of Job's friends and of course, Job himself. However, Job's faithfulness during these moments of trials must be commended as it would have been decisive to the latter manifestation of God's glory.

Therefore, if we, in sincerity, seek to be faithful to the gospel in our own struggles, weaknesses, confusions and trials, just like many holy men and women who went before us, we can be sure that God will manifest Himself through us and draw souls to Himself, just as on the cross, when all was accomplished, God revealed Himself in a very concrete way in Jesus and drew all souls to Himself.

Whilst we live here on earth as pilgrims looking for a city (Hebrews 11), we are to acknowledge, accept, live and witness to our hope amidst all scandals and contradictions within which the truth of our faith is and must be lived and witnessed to. Through them, the Christian's faith is truly tested, purified and comes alive. So that where our Head, Jesus, who was a contradiction, hated and despised by many, is, we too might, by His grace, attain an eternal rest from all our trials and sufferings. The attainment of this rest will indeed be the attainment of the true treasure of our heart, God, by whose power we have in the end overcome.

REFERENCES

1. Matt. 6:21
2. Lk 12:33
3. Matt. 13:44
4. Jer. 20:7
5. Jer. 20:9
6. Jn. 10:17-18
7. Phil. 3:8-14
8. Prov. 4:23
9. Col. 3:1-2
10. Col. 2:4,8,20
11. Col. 3:5-7, 12
12. Matt. 19:27
13. Ps 23:4, Ps 27:3,4
14. *Matt. 11:29*
15. Phil 2:5
16. Phil 2:6-7a
17. John 4:34

18. John 17:9-10
19. Hebrews 12:2
20. Søren Kierkegaard, *"Training in Christianity; And the Edifying Discourse which Accompanied it" Trans. By Walter Lowrie.* Princeton University Press, 2015. *Project MUSE* muse.jhu.edu/book/42828.
21. William McDavid, "Kierkegaard on (Lost) Offense of Christianity" 2016, Kierkegaard on the (Lost) Offense of Christianity - Mockingbird (mbird.com)
22. Matt. 11:30
23. 2 Corinthians 5:17
24. 1 John 3:9
25. Romans 7:17
26. Benedict XVI, Deus Caritas Est, (Rome: Libreria Editrice Vaticana, 2005, p.2
27. 1 John 4:8
28. John 1:5. In the prologue of John the Eternal Word that comes into the world, steeped in darkness, shines forth so brightly that it overpowers the darkness.
29. St Athanasius, *On Incarnation*, (Rome: Libreria Editrice Vaticana, 2005, p.1-57
30. St Athanasius, *On Incarnation,* Translated and edited by a Religious of SPCK, 2008, p.1-57

31. St Athanasius, *On* Incarnation, Translated and edited by a Religious of SPCK, 2008, P.6
32. Benedict XVI, *Deus Caritas Est*, (Rome: Libreria Editrice Vaticana, 2005 p.10
33. 1 John 4:19
34. Ephesians 1:3-14
35. Romans 5:6,10. St Paul presents in a very power way the gratuitousness of the Salvation in Christ, thus bringing out more clearly the unconditional character of God's love towards.
36. Romans 5:5

Printed in Great Britain
by Amazon